Alphabet Adventure

By Dawn Rundman
Illustrated by Linda Bronson

Hi! I'm Alfa the Ant. Can you find me on every page?

This book is for young children who are learning about their place in God's big family.

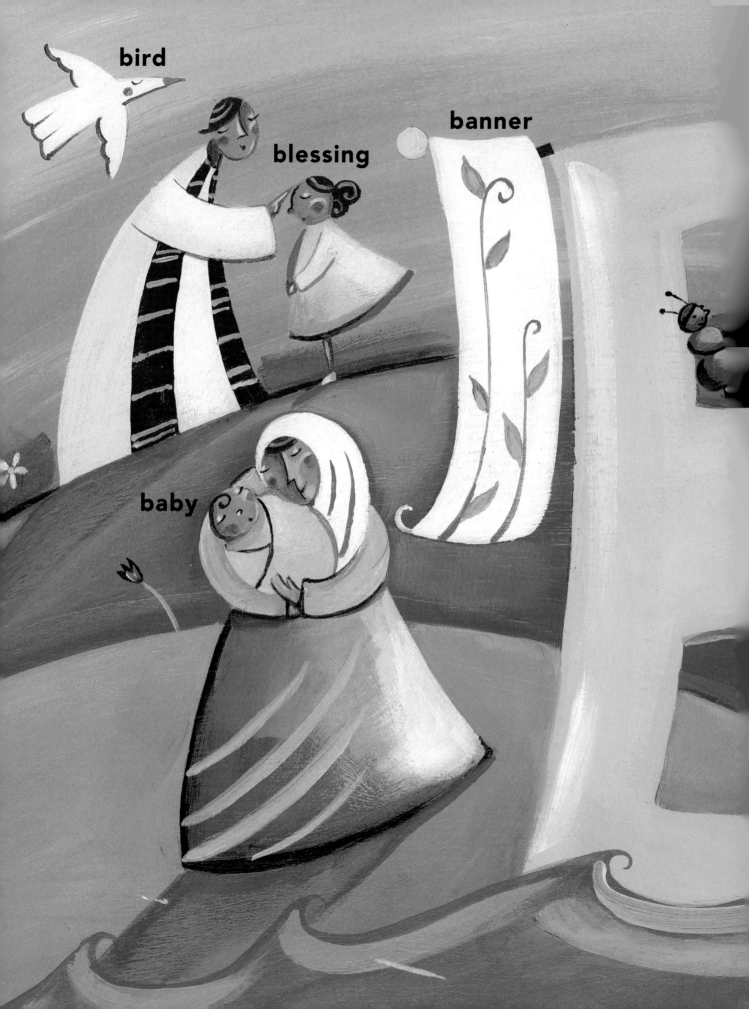

baptism

Bible

basket

disciples

D

day

daughters

dads

Earth

E

EVERYONE in the whole wide world

Francis of Assisi

friends and family

font

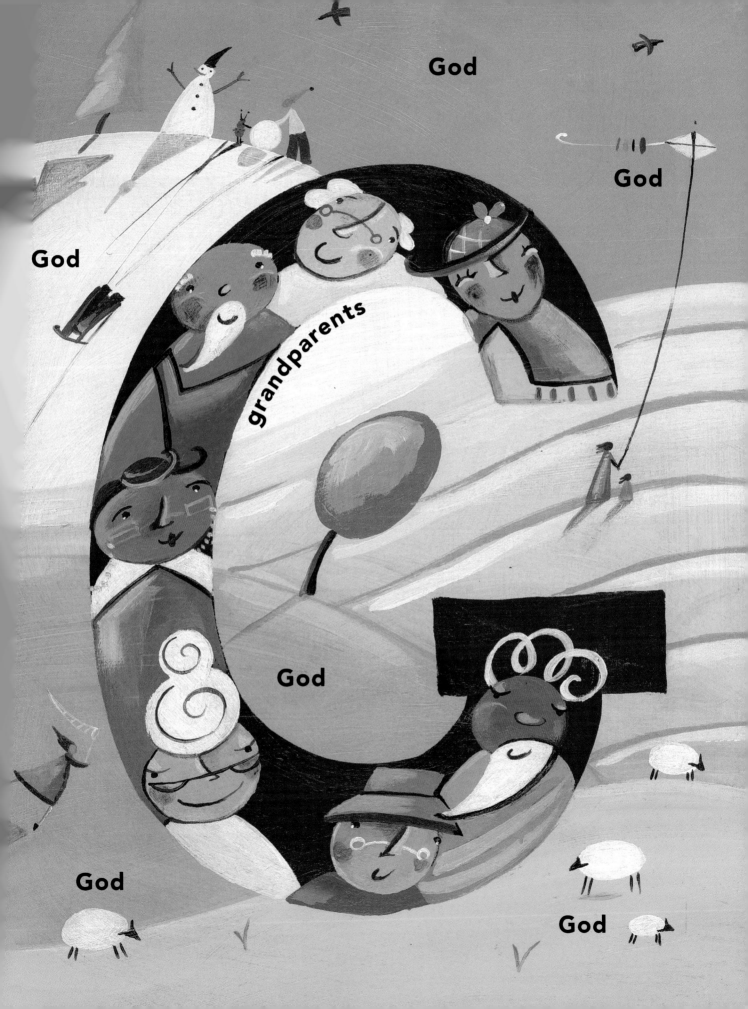

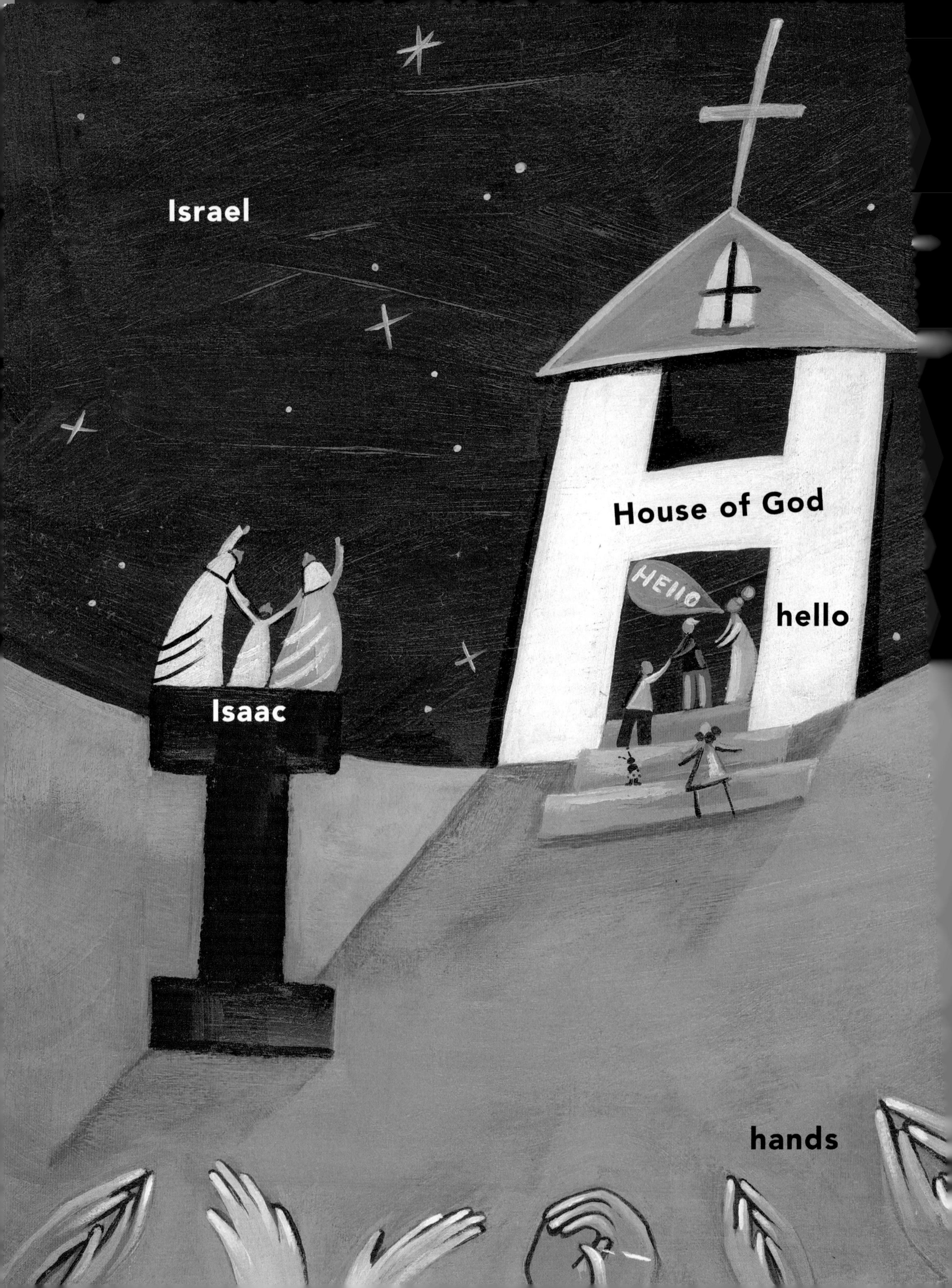
Israel
House of God
HELLO
hello
Isaac
hands

kiss

love

Lord's Supper

moon

Mary, mother
of Jesus

Mary and
Martha

Miriam
and
Moses

moms

night

Noah

neighborhood

neighbors

offering

pare

pets

pass the
peace

pray

pastors

quiet

uncles

volunteers

water

EXodus

YOU!

Zacchaeus

EliZabeth

Zechariah

Your Alphabet Adventure has just begun.
Find these things and people to continue the fun

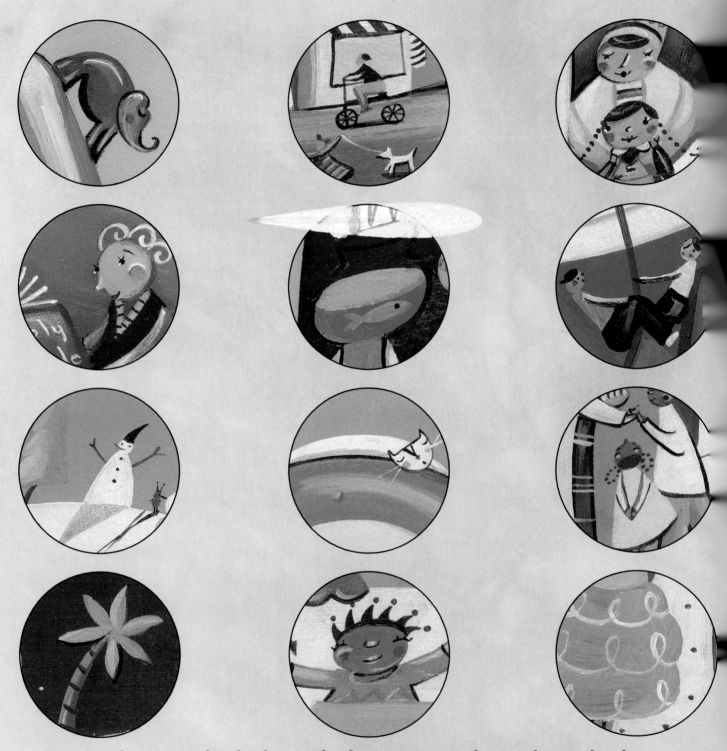

When you look through the pages, take a closer look.
These things appear more than once in this book!

- baby
- baptismal font
- bird
- book
- candle
- cross
- dog
- flower
- guitar
- hat
- sheep
- soccer ball
- star
- tree
- turtle
- watering can